I0438143

Plain Truth

By John Tait

PRESS

Contents

The Lost Republic

American government, in its natural state, served as Western civilization's crowning achievement; in its current state, it is our most devastating failure. The former represents an entity comprised of great men dedicated to protecting and preserving culture; the latter is made up of traitors' intent on its destruction. Whereas the Continental Congress declared independence despite certain war, contemporary government forces its citizens to relinquish basic rights in pursuit of conflicts.

Natural government, established through a desire for security, is based upon a nation's history, culture, and heritage. It can be neither forced nor enforced at the point of a gun but established through the people's will. While natural government is the result of a nation's past and optimism for the future, contemporary government ignores the former and devastates the latter. What was once an indispensable friend has become our most dangerous foe.

To examine how far removed from natural government we are, let us suppose history's greatest Western thinkers attempted to create an ideal government from nothing. Ignorant of contemporary government, the very idea of devising, let alone accepting, what has become common practice in Washington is inconceivable. While various forms of taxation would be accepted by some, proposing the current tax system would be absurd due to both its complexity and high rates. Not only allowing but pursuing a course of immigration consisting primarily of people from other cultures would be regarded as foolish. Proposing that those people would then be granted privileges not awarded to themselves or their posterity would be senseless. The government then authorizing that tax money to be distributed to the rest of the world, whether they immigrated to this new country or not, would be ridiculous. Government was created to protect society, not destroy it.

It is not necessary only to wonder about the results of such a meeting. Many of Western civilization's greatest men destroyed the remnants of monarchy and imperialism, allowing them the opportunity to create a government using only the most cherished aspects of our culture. The result was a government granted influence at the request of people who pursued like-minded goals. Whereas modern-day politicians work towards centralization of power in order to obtain influence, their predecessors pursued the difficult task of challenging history's most extensive empire. While our founders risked their lives to create freedom from monarchy, their contemporary counterparts pursue wealth at posterity's expense.

The unity evident allowed the end of foreign rule and creation of natural government. John Jay, in Federalist 2, mentioned the important role unity played: "Providence has been pleased to give this one connected country to one united people—a people descended from the same ancestors, speaking the same language, professing the same religion, attached to the same principles of government, very similar in their manners and customs, and who, by their joint counsels, arms, and efforts, fighting side by side throughout a long and bloody war, have nobly established their general liberty and independence." For natural government is the result of natural society; unnatural society is the result of contemporary government.

Being that a nation contains many more people than a simple gathering, it is necessary for a group of people to grant themselves representation through one or more people. Expectations of those representatives will be similar if members of the group share a common history, heritage, and culture. In that situation, every man will have a voice.

As a district becomes more diverse, its representative must fulfill expectations of people from different cultures with contradictory expectations. Those of a particular background will ask for special privileges. However, special privileges for one group always come at the expense of another. As the groups grow more substantial in both size and number, the representative's job will become increasingly more difficult. A politician expected to address the concerns of his constituents will find the task impossible.

This is a main culprit in the decline of our American republic. Representing the people properly has become impossible. One group demands privileges while another simply asks to be left alone. The solution sought by most has been to grant some of the requested privileges, which are always done at another's expense. The representative compromises both his duty to protect each constituent's property and also the founding principles on which our nation is based. It is in this age of false compromise in which those who request in abundance become the greatest benefactors while those who wish to be left alone have become regular victims of thievery.

The ideal form of government is simple, effective, and answers to those whom representatives are elected to serve. Government becomes less effective and its recipients forgotten as it grows more complex, often aiding foreigners at the expense of citizens.

Most modern governments share one similar advantage. They were produced and established through their own history, heritage, and culture while representing a particular hope for posterity. Mass colonization, caused in part by religious intolerance in England, resulted in our 1st Amendment granting freedom of religion. The horrors experienced by one or more generations often allow their descendants to enjoy greater freedom.

Under ideal circumstances, patriotism is a sign of strong citizenship. Under current conditions, it is proof of weakness. We have not grown since declaring and winning independence but have retreated back as control has left our hands and returned to a very few who are distant from society operating in a government that was originally organized into three separate branches. While well-designed by our founders, the following accurately describes contemporary reality:

1. An increasingly powerful executive branch led by the President.
2. An increasingly distant Congress, members of which identify and pursue favor within circles of influence.
3. The judicial system appointed by the 1st and approved by the 2nd.

The first two, controlled by an extremely exclusive organization, seek approval from elites representing much less than 1% of the population, contributing nothing of consequence to society. The third obtains power only at the request of the first two.

Therefore, the assumption that our system of checks and balances protects our best interests is laughable as they are independent of each other in design but not reality.

One must support three falsehoods in order to defend our current state of affairs:

1. That the executive and legislative branches act independently.
2. That the aforementioned branches of government act in our interests.

3. That the power behind the scenes will exercise only the authority to control two branches of government while ignoring the third. This, of course, is absurd considering that each is designed to share power with the other two.

Many Americans believe our system of checks and balances assures proper representation. If one branch pursues an unwise policy, passage would be avoided by the other two. That, of course, explains expectation rather than reality. One group controlling all three renders checks and balances useless. The result does not change despite the number of puppets on stage so long as those pulling the strings remain constant.

The composition of government has matched its actions regarding the rightful direction of scorn. Betrayal of one's countrymen has become a necessary trait, while loyalty results in being deemed unworthy to serve. Joining such an exclusive government shuts one off from the world that they have sworn to protect and into another which plans the destruction of those same people.

Thus, the system of checks and balances is rendered meaningless; one entity checking itself three times provides concrete evidence that contemporary American government is restrained equal to that of France when Louis XIV simply refused to call the Estates General.

Power in modern American society is centralized; orders now originate in Washington as opposed to London. When power is centralized with so few holding the reigns, one must promise first and prove shortly thereafter in order to obtain and keep any semblance of influence. The glorious cause for which our founders fought has been lost due to greed, apathy, and ignorance.

Americans, in defense of patriotism, reflect upon past achievements rather than contemporary success, as pride represents its source and logic its aspiration. Past achievement resulted from an informed citizenry voting in noble men representing good intentions. Contemporary America has witnessed uninformed subjects supporting foolish scoundrels. The result is power resting in the hands of very few, with those elected representing the demands of a tiny minority rather than the majority.

Despite modern-day patriotism being well-represented, the truth remains that American citizens are better served by the statesmen no longer living than the politicians in power today. In order to honor the precedence they established we have not only a right but also a duty to alter government to meet the needs of ourselves and posterity.

A great debate setting the course of our nation occurred between declaring independence and George Washington assuming the role of President. At the debates conclusion, a woman named Mrs. Powell asked Benjamin Franklin the outcome of those most consequential proceedings. Franklin said in response, "A Republic, if you can keep it!"

The challenge laid out by Franklin must be changed, as our duty is no longer to preserve but to re-establish, as natural government is a right of all people but a reality for so few. It is the fact that our Republic has been lost, a fear of our founders, which explains the necessity to examine our current state of affairs. Such a deficiency can be proven by government's determination in choosing an improper course of action with every decision.

Government, the entity that exists to make us safer, pursues a course that makes us constantly less so. We can do justice neither to ourselves or posterity while shackled and led down a path on which our founders are ridiculed instead of revered. Thus, the importance of identifying the cause, exploring the consequences, and discovering possible solutions is obvious.

Repression without Representation

Small nations are often subdued by their superiors in size, wealth, and prestige despite a significant will to preserve what is rightfully theirs. Powerful nations, ignorant of history, recede from grandeur resulting from internal betrayal. At our nation's founding, patriotism made good men heroes and great men legends. Today, good men have become voiceless and great men criminalized.

In more natural times, men considered worthy of great honor and respect were the protectors and preservers of country and culture. After eight years as President, George Washington ceded power, which was an extremely rare gesture at that point in Western civilization.

Today, power remains constant while varying individuals deceptively appear to acquire it. To reach such levels of phony respectability, it is often necessary to achieve membership within certain organizations in addition to supporting issues adverse to American interests.

Contrary to contemporary times, great men held positions of power during our nation's infancy. The result was the avoidance of war as opposed to its pursuit. During the XYZ Affair, Washington's successor, John Adams, resisted calls for war from both common citizens and members of his own party. He understood that preparations for war were necessary. Declaring war, on the other hand, was not. Even today, as military glory is not revered to the extent it was during his time, modern-day Presidents, without exception, have deployed forces to numerous foreign nations. We would do well to elect a commander-in-chief as rational as Adams.

The 2004 presidential election witnessed two men representing comparable ideologies and from similar backgrounds. Both were born into wealthy Northeastern families and later attended Yale. George Bush's grandfather had been a Unites States Senator representing Connecticut, while John Kerry is a member of the wealthy Forbes family on his mother's side. Additionally, both belong to Skull and Bones, which has roughly 800 living members at any given time. Is it not a coincidence that an organization represented by so few could call both major Presidential candidates members?

However, an organization exists slightly greater in number and substantially more significant in status which represents a much more dangerous threat. The first president to utilize such a group of perceived scholars was Woodrow Wilson. To do this, it is widely believed that a small group of men met privately in New York City and drafted the basis for Wilson's 14 Points. Less than five years later, in 1921, the Council of Foreign Relations became an official organization led by John W. Davis.

Wilson obtained and maintained power through good fortune, deception, and collaboration, which contemporary politicians continue to enjoy. The former experienced such fortune during the election of 1912 as a battle between Teddy Roosevelt and William Howard Taft broke the Republican stranglehold on the White House. Wilson's successors, on the other hand, often benefit from obtaining the right people's trust. As modern politicians are known for deceiving their fellow countrymen, Wilson provided the perfect example by winning re-election after keeping the United States out of the first three years of Europe's War without the intention to continue such a policy. Collaboration, exhibited by Wilson and explained in the previous paragraph, has been duplicated by all major modern political figures in a much more formal fashion. Just as those in front of the cameras exhibit similarities, Richard Haas carries the torch today for the original group, which holds vast power behind the scenes.

As Americans celebrated New Year's Day in 1994, a major step toward the existence of a North American Union came into effect. The North American Free Trade Agreement removed most existing tariffs between the United States, Canada, and Mexico while starting a process whereby all other taxes on imports would be phased out over the next 15 years. It must not be missed that the changes occurred over the course of 15 years. Change is less noticeable when it occurs over a longer period of time.

Less than four weeks earlier, President Clinton signed the agreement. Former Presidents Ford, Carter, and Bush attended the ceremony in a show of support, which unintentionally provided further evidence of their desire to witness the erosion of American sovereignty.

While introducing Clinton, Vice President Al Gore said, "There are some issues that transcend ideology. That is, the view is so uniform that it unites people in both parties. This means our country can pursue a bipartisan policy with continuity over the decades. That's how we won the Cold War. That's how we have promoted peace and reconciliation in the Middle East. And that's how the United States of America has promoted freer trade and bigger markets for our products and those of other nations throughout the world. NAFTA is such an issue."

The statement was notable not because the speech was performed so eloquently nor passage of the law so noble but because it provides tangible evidence that neither major party plans to defend American sovereignty. By their own admission, the Council on Foreign Relations has been pursuing their goal of forming a "One-World Government."

Just two years prior to the signing of NAFTA, CFR member and Deputy Secretary of State from 1994-2001 Strobe Talbott made the following cred-ible threat against American sovereignty: "In the next century, nations as we know it will be obsolete; all states will recognize a single, global authority. National sovereignty wasn't such a great idea after all." The idea is foreign to most private citizens, though it is an ordinary view among members of both the Council and government. Such an unfortunate fact renders the possibility of coincidence impossible.

The actual erosion of American autonomy by the executive branch has been underway for generations. Barry Goldwater, Ronald Reagan, and George W. Bush are the only non-CFR members to receive the Presidential nomination of either major party since Harry Truman occupied the White House. While Bush is not a member, the CFR is represented in the majority of his original and current staff. Among the most notable are Dick Cheney, Condoleezza Rice, Paul Wolfowitz, Colin Powell, and Donald Rumsfeld.

It is in the most influential cabinet positions where CFR members are most often found. There have been 14 Secretaries of State and Treasury and 11 at the Pentagon. Additionally, men who have led in the most notable recent major war efforts have been members, including Colin Powell, Wesley Clark, and David Petraeus.

Mere coincidence would be inconceivable if the list ended with the upper echelons of American government. However, their work within the government is only beginning.

According to the CFR official Web site, "One of the Council's main functions is to provide a nonpartisan forum for informed foreign policy debate." However, the debate seems to be closed.

The CFR controls not only the message but also the messengers. The most influential major network anchors are CFR members. Tom Brokaw, Barbara Walters, Diane Sawyer, Jim Lehrer, and Dan Rather are among the most well-known, comprising a lengthy list.

In addition to television, an extensive list of the most distributed newspapers and magazines are run under the direction of CFR members. The register includes *The Washington Post*, *Washington Times*, *Wall Street Journal*, *New York Times*, *U.S. News and World Report*, *Time*, *Newsweek*, and *National Review*.

The media also performed its part in promoting CFR members for the office of President during the 2008 primary season. Only its members were issued "top-tier" status. This includes Hillary Clinton, Barack Obama, John Edwards, Rudy Giuliani, and Fred Thompson.

The man they hope to succeed is an actual contributor at the meetings in which our nation's demise is planned. Thus far, the leaders of the North American countries have met on at least four occasions specifically to address the issue of a Union. The first occurred in March of 2005, shortly after Bush's second term began. A year later, the trio met in Cancun. In 2007, they met twice north of the border, with Felipe Calderon picking up right where former Mexican President Vicente Fox left off. The first conference took place in February in Ottawa followed by the infamous August meeting in Montebello.

When questioned about the intentions of the three national leaders, Bush called the creation of the North American Union "quite comical." However, the evidence proves otherwise. George Bush's old 2000 election ally and CFR member Kathryn Harris was the House sponsor of H.R. 2672, which is better known as The North American Cooperative Security Act. Its stated purpose is to "direct the Secretary of State to establish a program to bolster the mutual security and safety of the United States, Canada, and Mexico, and for other purposes."

The idea of one government consisting of three separate cultures has been attempted. Perhaps the most infamous example is Iraq. In 1921, the country of Iraq was created consisting of three distinct peoples: Sunnis in the center, Kurds to the north, and Shia in the south. The arrangement was made not by the people it would affect most but at the hands of British imperialists led by Prime Minister David Lloyd George.

In its earliest years, Iraq was held together by a brutal dictator representing the Sunnis and defended by the British. Chaos, violence, and bloodshed are still widespread almost nine decades later with no end in sight.

It must be asked how a group totaling less than 5,000 members could obtain such power despite pursuing objectives running contrary to our will. The answer is not through election, appointment, or any other noble means. It was formed in a similar manner to which its business is conducted today—through secrecy! Since new members are admitted only at the request of at least one current member and the pleasure of many, they have in fact set up a modern-day monarchy in which very few people obtain influence over the masses while passing on power to whomever they choose.

The Project for the New American Century is a more publicly outspoken offshoot of the CFR in which Jewish ancestry is preferred and loyalty to Israel essential. They hold much responsibility for establishing many of the Councils next steps. Ironically, these groups not only share ideas but also members. Signers of the original Statement of Principles for the interventionist group Project for the New American Century include Cheney, Rumsfeld, and Wolfowitz. Members of this organization believe that we have a responsibility as a nation "to challenge regimes hostile to our interests and values" and should play "a vital role in maintaining peace and security in Europe, Asia, and the Middle East".

PNAC is of the opinion that creating distant democracies with our values is worthy of American blood. It is, they believe, our way of life that is best for everyone. Of course, they fail to acknowledge that the best form of government depends on a nation's history, customs, and culture, which vary from people to people. A principled foreign policy recognizes that people have a different concept of the ideal society based on their own past. What is the point of having separate countries if a nation's culture is rendered meaningless by the most powerful, which forces their form of government on the world?

Such total control by so few in all areas of significance fuels ignorance. Both those who admit apathy or assume to understand the day's main issues are left in the dark. Many misinformed people direct efforts to impact issues that are only superficially significant.

A terrible tragedy is the difficulty experienced by honorable men attaining high office. To observe our nation disgraced and attempt to change its course results in being deemed unworthy of praise, whereas those who prove loyalty to influential yet repulsive organizations are rewarded. As the colonists learned before declaring independence, governments that need not face the people through elections are a much easier source from whom to take advantage.

Examining the loyalty of government, we find that allegiance is directed toward so few. As the following chapter illustrates, a thoughtful examination of government acts since the formation of the aforementioned organizations makes one believe that not even the most foolish among us would support such counter-productive legislation. To achieve their goal of one-world government, an attempt to make America look like the world is evident.

As time passes, it becomes increasingly easier to classify America as an oligarchy. While some continue to consider it a republic, the facts prove such faith illogical. The media, government, and select organizations obtaining all influence are causing us to transfer back to the days of monarchy and serfdom in which the expendable majority serves the interest of an exclusive minority. It was the demise of an imperialist monarchy in America and creation of a republic that the founders risked their fortunes and well-being to obtain. Ironically, we have returned to those unbearable circumstances not by force but through apathy and ignorance.

Over the past half century, six Republicans and four Democrats have occupied the White House. Several times during that period, the source of perceived power switched hands. However, change, if it occurred at all, was minimal. Both parties have been guilty of increasing taxes, spending, and government authority while waging counter-productive war. While we suffered the consequences in wasted money and lost lives, those obtaining tangible power reaped the rewards. As is the case in which government is run by thieves, our nation's inheritance is plundered at posterity's expense.

In America, the President is busy promoting unnecessary wars, increasing his perceived influence, and weakening our culture, which is part of our national erosion. His pursuit of power comes at the expense of everyone, for world government enslaves mankind. It is unfortunate when the man least worthy of respect holds the title that people most revere.

Crimes of the Government

The following chapter is full of unfortunate facts that make liberty and freedom fictional for contemporary Americans and in great peril for posterity. While analyzing the evidence, I offer clear arguments, simple logic, and the plain truth.

Much has been written and argued regarding most of today's important issues. The arguments have been made by people of various philosophies with conflicting desires. However, those debates were irrelevant. Their desires stemmed from duty to globalism and adherence to political correctness. Our survival demands a shift regarding the debate's focus to culture, history, and nationalism.

Two choices lay before us. We can either realize our duty or subsist without regard to posterity. The former makes us heroic to future generations. The latter leaves contemporary Americans rightfully regarded as traitorous.

A more noble cause could never be undertaken. Our course of action does not only affect the living but also those of the past and future. We can vindicate the work of our ancestors while creating an extraordinary future for our descendants. If we choose to wait, America will suffer the fate of its predecessors, and tyranny will conquer the tree of liberty planted by our founders. Confrontation, however, allows the unborn an opportunity to live in freedom enjoying the fruits of our labor.

Much has been said in defense of our current course. It is of absolute necessity that we analyze opposing arguments in order to fully comprehend the destruction that present policy has inflicted upon us. Concurrently, we must understand that continuing such policies causes further harm to ourselves and our country.

According to former President Clinton, our country will be without a majority race by 2050. Members of both the media and government have commented that the aforesaid statement is inevitable. The PEW report released earlier this year stated that such a day will occur three years prior to Clinton's prediction. Our posterity will reflect upon us with abomination if that statement becomes fact by mid-century.

By referring to America as a multi-ethnic society, an attempt is made to deny all notions of culture, history, and heritage. America's origins are no longer understood as the greatest example of concurrence, prosperity, and habitation. It has been dishonored as the most appalling nightmare of dissidence, scarcity, and subjugation.

There is perhaps no better judge of the future than the past. As we choose our future, no policy is more important than immigration. It is one of the few issues in which government officials use history in their defense through the overused "Nation of Immigrants" mantra. However, they only acknowledge the facts necessary to suit their purpose as they accept part of history but ignore the rest.

It is often said that Spanish will surpass English as the most spoken language in America within a few decades' time. After this initial statement, it is common to hear reference to adaptation; such as the benefit regarding business opportunities. However, the answer is not adaptation but prevention. The latter demonstrates strength and affection while the former represents weakness and disloyalty. Adaptation to change that obliterates our nation is treasonous. Why should we adapt to a source of our own demise while being greater in both number and power?

Many have stated that diversity is the source of our strength. Nations composed of one race, culture, and religion are somehow weak, fragile, and worthy of our disdain. If it is diversity that has made America so strong, I feel the need to pose a question that has been avoided for far too long. How can a sovereign nation such as America produce its strength from the characteristics of the world's other nations?

The answer is sure to revolve around the false assumption that America was never created almost entirely by Christian Europeans predominantly from

England who spoke the same language. However, nothing could be further from the truth. Had the inhabitants been generally Japanese with other Asian nations representing the remaining population, no doubt exists that American history would differ drastically. The language of choice would be Japanese as opposed to English, and the two prevalent faiths would be Shinto and Buddhism instead of Christianity. The foundation of America would be based upon Asian culture as a substitute for Western civilization. Differences among nations within the same continent are always noticeable and sometimes drastic. Language, culture, heritage, history, and physical appearance are just some of the existing disparities between nations on any given continent. Compare two nations on different continents, and the discrepancies become more drastic and obvious.

Christianity enhanced Jefferson's argument in favor of rebellion against a power autocracy and forming a government that would protect our God-given rights. Of almost equal significance, the previous establishment of "separation of powers" throughout much of Europe aided in forming our republic. To deny the facts surrounding our founding is not mere ignorance of American culture but a calculated effort to misinform society of its past in order to change our future.

The fact remains that America's founding would have been impossible without previous documents and philosophy upon which Western civilization was built. As admitted by our founders, Western philosophers, most notably John Locke, were instrumental in both the decision to declare independence and the outcome upon victory in that monumental battle.

Thomas Jefferson admitted such when purchasing three portraits of the men he revered above all others: Francis Bacon, Isaac Newton, and Locke. In defending his reason for the purchase, Jefferson said that they are "the three greatest men who have ever lived, without any exception." Jefferson and his contemporaries looked toward great Western men, not world figures.

Examples, in addition to admission, can also prove the importance of Western culture regarding our nation's founding. In the century preceding the American Revolution, Locke declared life, liberty, and property basic rights, ideas later espoused by our founders. He not only impacted our national and various state documents but advocated for separation of powers and understood the obligation for revolution against tyranny.

Such confusion is caused by poor policy that runs contradictory to our history. An allowed invasion from the South, being one of our government's most disappointing failings, is exceeded in scope by its less discussed counterpart—legal immigration. While the invasion represents an unwillingness to protect our culture, current legal immigration policy is an outright denial of our heritage.

The world is full of countries representing conflicting interests aggravated by history and geography. We have suffered from a similar problem with our southern neighbors. Their false teaching of history has left millions angry about the past while seeking revenge in the future. Any consequences we suffer are our own doing as we possess the means to prevent any reaction. However, such is not the case in the Middle East, where we anger a billion people for the sake of a few million. As we pursue such policies in ignorance, common sense pleads for neutrality. We have been blessed with 5,000 miles of distance from the source of inevitable warfare. To pursue war when blessed with such fortune is to choose danger when safety is more easily attained.

As with individuals, each nation is unique. Japan suffered severe consequences by failing to recognize the American character during WWII. A nation can also commit suicide by failing to recognize itself. Designers and supporters of 1965's Immigration Act were not inventors but imitators of England's failed immigration policy of the 1950's. There can be wisdom in duplicating productive policies, but nothing could be more foolish than doing such with established policy that has already proven destructive. As the British did during the prior decade, American government tried to turn us into what we are not instead of what we had always been. Nations that attempt to subjugate others become captors rather than masters. Under current conditions, such a conclusion is inevitable. Most Western governments, through their actions, are pursuing such a result.

While most fight against the demise of their own nation, our government pursues such by passing legislation. The Immigration Act of 1965 was passed by Congress and signed by Lyndon Johnson without regard to our nation's foundation. For the first time, American immigration policy had completely changed course in favor of non-Europeans. History has proven Ted Kennedy's statement that "the ethnic mix of this country will not be upset" to be fraudulent. Common sense, not time, was the original indicator that drastically changing immigration policy to restrict traditional immigrants in favor of non-westerners would upset the balance referred to by Kennedy.

As part of the Immigration Act of 1990, the Diversity Visa Lottery program was instituted to allow for 55,000 "diversity immigrants" to obtain citizenship. In twenty-five years, the government went from disguising to declaring their long-term agenda. In defending such policies, both government and civilian supporters of mass immigration deny the existence of an American culture by pointing to the differences between our cities and regions. While I do admit that some differences exist, I reject their denial of an American culture. It is true that obvious differences exist between Boston, New York, and various small towns throughout the Midwest. However, parallel distinctions would be apparent by a visitor to Oxford, London, and a small English town near the Scottish border. To deny the existence of our culture on that rationale is a rejection of all national societies.

It is highly necessary to examine the issue of cultural diversity given the increased existing evidence that has accumulated since passage of the aforementioned Immigration Act. Within diverse societies, a hero of one group is often despised by the others. Christopher Columbus provides a worthy example. Every year, Denver has a parade in honor of Columbus for his major role in making Western man aware of what would later become American soil. Such a monumental achievement has earned Columbus his own national holiday. However, scorn is directed toward his legacy by a large group of dissenters.

The father of our country provides another example of American heroes being despised within our own nation. New Orleans adopted an anti-slave owner policy that resulted in a school named after George Washington being renamed with Charles Drew. Another revered Virginian, Robert E. Lee, had his name taken down from a school and replaced with that of Ronald McNair. Two giants of American history have been excluded from proper acknowledgement and replaced with minor figures in black history. Diversity celebrates difference, while nations are based upon similarities.

As the following examples prove, diversity leads to physical threats against citizens in addition to crimes against culture. This past November marked the third straight in which France was afflicted with heavy violence. All three cases were predictably similar. The perpetrators were all African and/or Muslim, occurred after an event in which individuals of the aforementioned race and religion were thought to be mistreated, and took place in the "no-go" areas surrounding Paris. The mainstream politicians blamed opposing parties and a lack of financial aid in minority neighborhoods for the riots. French elder statesman Jean Marie Le Pen predicted that the French people would pay a high cost for negligent immigration policy. After the first set of November riots, Le Pen said that it "could be the first signs of a civil war." Two years later, the French witnessed three consecutive nights of rioting, resulting in dozens of burning cars and over 100 injured police officers. It appears that Le Pen was right. The 2005 riots were the first of many. Le Pen's defense of his nation throughout a lengthy career in public life prevented him from participating in a 2002 presidential debate with Jacques Chirac and possibly from attaining the Presidency. While Le Pen's courage denied him the opportunity to occupy a deserved office, others have actually lost their jobs despite a display of heroism.

In Malmo, Sweden, policeman Bengt Linstrom lost his job for publicly criticizing the consequences of mass immigration. Linstrom has witnessed the consequences intensify as the city's demographics shift towards a Swedish minority. In addition to firing Linstrom, the Malmo police department warned his former co-workers to keep their mouths shut or suffer the same fate.

The targets in France and Sweden are often professionals entering areas due to work necessities. However, civilians were targeted in the most notorious attack on Britain. On July 7th, 2005, four Muslim suicide bombers killed 52 innocent people and caused injury to another 700.

While the previous examples link racial diversity and physical threats to individuals, the following demonstrate the vulnerability of the state itself. Less than two decades ago, the largest country on earth broke into 15 separate nations. A strong central government that controlled nearly every aspect of life could only hold an ethnically diverse people together so long. They chose to form their own nations based upon nationality rather than be held together through philosophy.

A thousand miles west and 17 years later, Belgium is suffering from a similar experience. The north has ties to the Dutch, while the south is French in ethnicity. Tension between the two remains high despite a cooling effect occurring after Yves Leterme was finally sworn into office after an almost 10-month period in which Belgium was very close to splitting in two. The question is no longer whether Belgium will split but when and through what means.

The U.S. is experiencing similar problems that are more obvious in certain communities. Many legal U.S. citizens advocate the secession of the American Southwest. They do not advocate the creation of its own nation but that it becomes part of their native homeland. With time and increasing numbers, Mexicans with or without legal status become more outspoken, a result of which was a 2005 billboard promoting a Spanish language newscast, which read, "Los Angeles, Mexico."

Many proponents of diversity have enjoyed the good fortune of living away from the neighborhoods they tout; the costs are not evident on a daily basis, making them ignorant of America's fragile state. Just like most cowards, they leave others to suffer the consequences of their actions. It is not they who must reside in once habitable cities such as Detroit, Youngstown, and much of Los Angeles. Their children won't be destined to suffer the same educational fate of those who attend once great schools in Atlanta, Birmingham, and Little Rock, which have been destroyed by the effects of desegregation, mass immigration, and nationally controlled schools. The inhabitants of the less fortunate neighborhoods within those cities have been left two undesirable choices: stay despite obvious danger or desert the place they call home. In either case, the ideal situation, the right of all people to obtain and a duty of ours to preserve, is ruined by those who act while ignorant of the results.

While the consequences of diversity are not sudden and apparent to simple observers, they are both obvious and dangerous to those who examine the issue closely. Let us assume that a proposal was discussed during the Cold War's height advocating the immigration of 100 million Communist Russians. Certainly, many questions would arise. Will they blend into American society? To whom will they pledge allegiance? Will "democracy" and "freedom" remain, or will America become a Communist state? The result of such immigration would surely make us more diverse. However, would we be better off? As the most severe consequences stared the people in the face, it would be widely agreed that the result of such policy would leave America less safe and more fractured. At the root of those concerns would be a desire to preserve our distinct American heritage. The consequences of diversity are much more apparent when they affect the living as opposed to the unborn.

Even before America existed as a sovereign nation, examples exist in which the colonists set a precedent expressing their desire to remain safe. It had been common practice for England to send criminals to the colonies as punishment for their crimes. Understanding the negative consequences on the colonies, both Virginia and Maryland passed laws against such importation. However, Parliament overrode those wishes in 1717, resulting in the transportation of over 30,000 convicts prior to the Revolution.

After gaining independence, protecting citizens from unnecessary consequences became a duty of government. Upon arrival at Ellis Island, potential immigrants were checked for illness. Those who did not threaten the well-being of American citizens were welcomed. Others who could potentially pass on disease were sent home. Representatives understood that immigration should never be a burden upon the American people.

The immigration example is only one method of drastically changing America. It is a slow process in which change is rarely felt as politicians use patience to their advantage and our detriment. This allows for great change in every aspect of our country to develop in a manner that does not upset the masses.

All nations have a clear set of principles that guide their actions, but no two share an identical philosophy. No law is meant for all people. Some nations are better off under a monarchy that dictates many laws, while others must witness people allowing few laws from elected officials. Imitation among nations forces people to be who they are not. You cannot make an American out of an Iraqi, just as an Iraqi can't become an American. That has been attempted by force in the former and invitation in the latter. Through such unwise policies, the American empire will aspire to conquer Iraq but could find itself conquered. Just as those who oppress others change the political landscape, so too do immigrants in their adopted homeland. The new arrivals are incompatible with the laws, rendering the situation ideal for no one and dangerous for everyone.

While current legal immigration policy is a reflection of poor legislation, the consequences of illegal immigration are increased by government's failure to act. The Mexican government, by its own admission, continues to promote a takeover of the American southwest. A multitude of benefits, porous southern border, and the opportunity for eventual citizenship make it appear as if both governments are working together toward such a conclusion. Their ultimate goal, called "reconquista," includes either all or part of 11 different states returning to Mexican control. A constitutionally mandated duty is ignored despite the enemy being obvious and the threat admitted.

Only two possible explanations can be made by government to explain their failure to address the issue. Either they are unable or unwilling. The former proves them not qualified, the latter disloyal. Eliminating the former is quite easy considering the worldwide tasks in which they have chosen to partake. A 1,952-mile impenetrable fence has been proposed for a sum of $50 million. While that may seem costly to some, it equals the cost of 7 hours of the war in Iraq or 10 months defending South Korea. If those costly and disadvantageous commitments can be made, it seems as though fulfilling a much less expensive constitutional duty is highly necessary. Unfortunately, the actions of government speak plainly enough: the security of Iraq and Korea is more important than that of the United States.

Few acts throughout history can be regarded as foolish and cowardly as bribing one's own conquerors. Such has become common practice from Washington elites. Members of both major parties spoke at the National Council of La Raza 2007 convention. At this time, the presidential nominees of both major parties plan to speak at the 2008 affair. A majority of La Raza's members support endless amnesty, mass additional immigration from Mexico, and the transfer of most of our Southwest to Mexico. Those who invade and demand receive sincere promises, while citizens who wish comfort and security are ridiculed.

Just as certain laws are not destined for all people, republican government is not appropriate for all nations. Some nations are not capable of creating and maintaining a republic. However, it is foolish for people to create such a government, thrive under those conditions, and then choose a course that their ancestors deemed intolerable. Many born slaves risk their lives in pursuit of freedom; but being born free and choosing slavery is inconceivable for ourselves, and we deprive posterity of their natural rights in the process.

The study of recent American history proves the concept of "blowback" to be an accurate drawback of many current policies. Unintended consequences are often the result of globalist adventures but also present themselves as possibilities domestically. The most ironic potential consequence to illegal immigration is that we may lose Texas in the same fashion in which it was obtained. Shortly after gaining independence from Spain in 1821, Mexico offered cheap land to American Protestants under two conditions in what would later become Texas. They had to claim loyalty to both Mexico and the Catholic Church. Of course, they did so only in word but not in truth. What began as 300 American immigrants in 1822 became a massive slow influx resulting in whites outnumbering Mexicans five to one at the War's onset in 1835. A year later, Sam Houston was sworn in as the first President of Texas. We gained Texas through the foolish immigration policies of Mexico. Government members, if honest, have proven themselves to be ignorant of their own history.

In order to delegitimize our stake in America, many have claimed that Mexico is the rightful owner of the Southwest and Indians everything else. It is said that white Americans' brutally killed the unlucky, while the fortunate were forced westward. However, that argument can only be made by those with little or no knowledge of world history.

Throughout the centuries, the world map has changed drastically. Many nations have witnessed drastic increases or decreases in size, while others have ceased to exist. No country has seen a greater expansion in size than Russia. As the 16th century began, Russia had reached the Ural Mountains to the East and was several hundred miles from Sea to the south. Within four centuries, its citizens were settling hundreds of miles past the Urals and didn't stop moving south until they reached the Black and Caspian Seas.

While Russia grew in size and strength, other nations either decreased significantly or diminished entirely. During the 18th century alone, Poland went from a European power to the victim of a partition that left its future existence uncertain. During their time of turmoil, our nation was beginning the process that made "Manifest Destiny" a reality.

The transformation of the world map is a historical process that may never end. Some claim that our nation's foundation is tainted and rightful ownership of its land belongs to both Indians and Mexico. If one is to follow that argument, they must also question the rightful existence of every single nation. Otherwise, the question must be asked, to which year should we go back?

Some state that we are in a battle between freedom and "Radical Islam." It is admitted that Muslims and Christians have substantial ideological differences. The facts prove that those differences have resulted in war on various occasions. However, no major disagreement between a Muslim nation and the United States occurred before Israel's creation, as we are separated by 5,000 miles and oceans on both sides.

Many have made the case that Muslim hatred is directed towards us simply due to our culture. They are, it is said, two completely different cultures that cannot co-exist. It is admitted that hatred has resulted from significant differences between people. However, the root cause of such hatred by so many people does not result from simple differences between those of dissimilar nations and religions. It is negative consequences caused by an aggressor and inflicted upon the victims. We have used their land for our military bases, American-led blockades have caused the starvation of millions, and our government has supported their enemy without reserve. They view our bases as desecration of their sacred land, have witnessed their fellow Muslims starved to death, and are conscious of our efforts in aiding Israel. Are we to believe that Muslims view those consequences as irrelevant and instead use cultural differences to urge hatred directed towards the West?

In defense of Middle Eastern involvement, many have unconvincingly made the case that refusing to attack their nations will result in war on American soil. Two main reasons prove their argument to be fallacious and display the foolish nature of government policy:

1. The reason for such hatred is our involvement in their affairs.
2. After causing anger, our government offers an invitation for citizenship.

It has become common to hear that we are hated because of our freedom. I will ignore the obvious mistake pertaining to our freedom, as this entire book denies any such assumption and instead focuses on the cause of hatred. It is not simple differences that cause hatred but negative consequences inflicted upon others that result from our actions. It is foolish to assume that cultural differences are the cause of such tension after establishing military bases, ordering blockades that result in mass starvation, and bombing their countries.

Men possess a natural desire to feel that they are protecting the women and children in their respective societies. This is certainly true in such relationships as father and child and husband and wife. When foreign troops enter the scene through force, male adults are likely to feel a sense of embarrassment, failure, and frustration that can lead to a disdain or even a strong hatred for the foreign troops.

When represented by a republic, two main reasons exist that explain the avoidance of war until it is absolutely necessary. First, the people are properly represented by statesmen who understand that the interest of the people and that of the state are identical. Second, the desires of both are not subservient to global aspirations. Our false republic has pursued unnecessary war with the urgency of an ancient monarch seeking military glory. Both look down upon those in battle as expendable in pursuit of their own selfish goals. International governments are constantly at war; the desire for increased world influence exceeds any will to protect one's fellow citizens. As history has proven, those who attempt to conquer the world are always conquered in the end. Globalism is incompatible with republican government.

The right of the strongest is no right at all, as ability is no excuse for immoral actions. American government, against better judgment, ignores such advice. Force is used by the more powerful, not the virtuous. When government pursues such an unfortunate course, it does so unconstitutionally. The oath they take is a promise to defend America at home, not spread democratic values abroad. A result of which is soldiers being forced to partake in actions threatening to the constitution they vow to uphold.

A conflict of interest exists in any republic that pursues empire. Force is based on the will of the strongest, while republican government suggests that the majority leads while the minority remains influential. The former allows one voice to speak, while the latter encourages many. If force means everything, right means nothing. The contradiction is obvious, and an unintentional admission of long-term goals is evident. It is an unfortunate change when a nation founded by resisting force to establish freedom embraces the former and destroys the latter.

From our Revolution an example of what America once was and what it has now become is evident. We are no longer fighting a grand war to establish liberty but have become a country in unending and unnecessary foreign conflicts resembling the Hessians of 18th Century Germany. Both soldiers have been led to war with no concern for themselves or their country. While the Hessians had the least alluring jobs, American soldiers have the most dangerous. Due to unnecessary foreign intervention, the Hessians were despised by the revolutionaries. Likewise, the Iraqis generally possess the same feelings toward American soldiers. German princes sent their countrymen over the Atlantic to engage in a long and difficult war for profit. Many who pursued the current war have become wealthy despite the many drawbacks. Perhaps most notably, the Hessians lost lives due to the perceived interest of Great Britain, while Americans suffer to benefit Israel. It is impossible to win an unnecessary war. Such wars are lost when the first penny is spent.

It has been said by many within our government that our existence depends on that of Israel. However, history has proven otherwise as our nation prospered in the seventeen decades in which we existed alone. What affect can a nation smaller in size and lesser in population than New Jersey have on our existence? No other nation can claim greater responsibility for Israel's birth and well-being. Many who proclaim the fragile nature of our state from either the pulpit or pen point to America as the father and Israel its favorite son. The question must then be asked, what father is dependent upon his son? When asking such, it becomes obvious that our government considers us as a subordinate which is subservient to its own dependent. The illogical nature of such theories reveals government's true intentions.

We have, according to both governments, become great friends due to our common pursuit of freedom and democracy. It is, they say, a relationship of natural attachment in which both sides benefit equally. However, the facts prove otherwise, as we give money, sweat, and blood while receiving nothing of consequence. I know of no example in which one side of a friendship is the only benefactor with the other being the lone recipient.

It has become common knowledge that our government gives a combined $3 billion per year in economic and military aid. While that may be true, it only represents a small percentage of the total cost to maintain our friendship. Our total expenditures in the Middle East will total over $1 trillion when factoring the cost of the Iraq War, the 11 functioning military bases in the aforementioned country, and several other bases throughout the region. That money must be factored in our donations to Israel since it is spent defending their interests at our expense.

When friendship between two nations is authentic, as opposed to fabricated, I know of no example in which one nation's enemy is the other's ally. However, Jonathan Pollard, while having been convicted of espionage against the United States, is regarded as a national hero in Israel. He is both celebrated by the Israeli people and defended by their government for transferring classified U.S. defense information to the nation in which he is loyal.

Although the Pollard incident was a terrible display of ingratitude, the attack on the USS Liberty in 1967 can be regarded as the most severe attack against the United States by a supposed ally. Israel seeks physical protection in addition to generous financial aid. It is common to hear contemporary American politicians issue a promise of swift justice to any nation that commits a major attack upon Israel. That promise, I am certain, would be met.

Forgiveness was given, however, when our government's favorite country attacked the American military. High-level officials and many soldiers onboard stated that the Israeli's engaged in an attack upon the USS Liberty. On June 8th, 34 Americans were killed while another 174 were wounded. The motive is clear: given that Israel was at war with Egypt, an understanding of late 19th and early 20th century American history reveals an obvious motive. Israel believed an attack upon the American military would result in a declaration of war against Egypt. In 1898, an explosion on the USS Maine caused popular support for war against Spain. Throughout most of WWI, the majority of Americans strongly desired exclusion from Europe's war until the Lusitania and other ships were attacked and the contents of the Zimmerman Telegram became public knowledge. Less than a quarter century later, despite the desire of President Roosevelt and a major pro-war propaganda machine, America avoided war until Pearl Harbor led to an instant increase in popular support along with a Congressional Declaration of War against Japan. The Israeli government, based upon our history, knew the proper route that would garner American support for their cause. Fortunately, no such declaration was made against Egypt, as it was discovered that Israel was guilty and their enemy innocent.

Government was created to protect us from enemies. Those observing its current actions without knowledge of American history are certain to observe its intention to create enemies. We have lost thousands of lives, spent trillions of dollars, established dozens of functioning military bases, and created enemies in the hundreds of millions. While that may benefit Israel, what have we achieved for ourselves?

We witness daily examples of the government's intentional destruction of American jobs. No more disgraceful instance exists than one that occurred in December 2003. George Bush, only days after visiting steel mill workers, removed the tariffs that protected their jobs. Shortly after and through the present day, Bush continues to claim that protectionism brought severe consequences. However, the opposite is true. Since shifting from the protective tariff to pursuing free trade, our trade surplus has become a deficit, while manufacturing towns have been decimated. The nation, which once produced 96% of all domestically consumed products, now imports nearly 70% of its goods. Adding insult to injury of all manufacturers, our current executive declared protectionism a thing of the past. That, however, must be considered par for the course. We are no longer self-sufficient regarding sovereignty, protecting ourselves, or making everyday decisions. Why should it come as a surprise when government destroys jobs and proclaims their permanent demise?

Counterproductive American politicians often espouse policies that are the exact opposite of those supported by our founders. Such is the case regarding trade in general and NAFTA in particular. The revolutionaries fought an empire possessing a greater economy, population, and perceived power in order to establish sovereignty despite threat of death. Their modern-day counterparts voluntarily cede such authority to nations that are inferior in wealth, number, and actual strength despite our best interests. Americans are forced to follow laws imposed by foreign bureaucrats making NAFTA a trade treaty in name that results in the relinquishment of sovereignty.

While NAFTA forces us to indirectly finance our sovereignty's demise, the United Nations achieves the same goal in a more obvious fashion. To obtain the benefit of allowing foreign people and countries to make our laws, we pay 22% of all U.N. budget funds. We have come a long way since the Revolution; we no longer forbid through force but welcome with fiscal support the demise of our liberty, sovereignty, and independence.

Within society, limits exist regarding the proper amount of authority one may exert over another. Consequences exist for a teacher who is either too strict or lenient. The former will negatively affect the students' will and the latter their ability. As with educators, government must exert its proper level of authority in order to establish its ideal influence. Government too weak can leave its citizens vulnerable to foreign threats; when too strong, government itself becomes the threat.

Re-establishment is an idea rarely discussed despite instant rewards. In order for consideration to

increase, a plan must be presented explaining immediate results, all of which would increase individual
freedom based upon Western history, heritage, and
culture. Sovereignty would be restored, allowing
American citizens to pursue additional changes and
address more complicated concerns:

1. All members of the executive, legislative,
   and judicial branches of government must
   be immediately recalled.
2. Issue a public proclamation declaring the
   United States a republic Western in heritage
   and guided by Christian principles.
3. The immediate repeal of all Immigration
   Acts enacted since 1965.
4. Abolishment of the Federal Reserve and re-
   institution of the gold standard.
5. The immediate repeal of all income tax laws,
   including the 16th Amendment.
6. Closing of all foreign military bases within
   1 year.
7. Massive placement of U.S. troops on
   our southern border until construction
   of an impenetrable double layer fence is
   complete.
8. Removal of the U.S. from all "free trade"
   treaties.
9. Immediately end all foreign aid.
10. Immediate withdrawal from the United
    Nations and NATO.

11. Abolishing the Department of Education and all federal mandates regarding the aforesaid to ensure local control of schools.
12. All laws depriving citizens of 2nd Amendment rights must be immediately abolished.
13. Declare all affirmative action programs and quota systems immediately null and void.
14. Add the phrase, "No Amendment to the Constitution may grant authority to government at the people's expense" to the Constitution.

I offer all advocates of our current state to name one reason in defense of pursuing our current course. Such is offered with full confidence, as not a single advantage will result. Despite the belief of some, being viewed positively abroad is not the path to surrender.

Prolonging our current condition guarantees a state of war, making enemies of our natural friends to whom the American people direct affection despite our government displaying contempt towards them. It is in our interest to avoid war and conflict throughout the world, which is impossible while alliances are kept with nations not blessed as we are with the fortune of good geography.

Office seekers, media members, and private citizens have proven that various opportunities exist to obtain fame and fortune resulting from controlled government. It is out of necessity, not selfish pursuits, that I espouse the little discussed concept of re-establishment. In doing so, I immediately make enemies with those guilty of making great men infamous and foolish men immortal. It is, without question, in the interest of ourselves and posterity. If we choose apathy over reason, common sense, and hard work, we will look upon these days with great regret while wondering what would have resulted from pursuing the most important task of our lives.

The loyalty of American government to foreign interests must end, or we will cease to exist. It is impossible to do the unborn justice while pursuing counterproductive policies and ignoring issues of utmost importance. As parents, we must not relish in minor individual success while wasting our ancestors' accomplishments at posterity's expense. The good we do individually will benefit our children not at all if they are without a country of their own. As further examination of the facts proves, we cannot meet our duty if we bequeath to our children a government that wastes their lives to benefit our destroyer.

A republic based upon Western values is our natural right. When Americans understand the facts and precarious nature of our time, action will be the decision and re-institution of a proper republic the goal. Most will surely realize our very traditional yet urgent needs when contemplating the reality of such unfavorable prospects. Waiting ensures continued rule by tyrants that will prolong the process whereby our rights are suppressed until not only they are nonexistent but so is any individual capable of re-instituting liberty. Should we continue on our current course, we are pursuing the suicide not only of ourselves but of our entire heritage as well.

Loyalty to government is understandable in some circumstances and noble in others. However, it is neither under current conditions. We are reduced in number and weakened regarding influence with each passing day. Waiting ensures that our ability to act will contract as the reasons for our dissatisfaction increase.

The Sleeping Giant

I t is extremely rare to meet a common citizen strong and sincere in the belief that America is headed in the right direction, which makes conceivable the idea of successful separation from our current course and instituting natural government.

All men blessed with the qualities of honesty and thoughtfulness are certain to conclude that positive change is necessary, though disagreement concerning its urgency may exist. However, the time for action is before us. Both the magnitude of the crimes committed against us and certainty that our strength in numbers is only a temporary benefit under current circumstances make today the perfect time to respond. Inaction ensures that the chains clamped to our children will be heavier than those with which we are currently overwhelmed.

Those chains, however, are not necessary; we are neither suppressed by a force greater in number nor imposed upon by a foundation of abuse. We must defend ourselves through arguments in favor of logic, history, and common sense. Our nation was founded and established as a republic that repelled harsh foreign rule that has been imposed upon us once again. When considering the vast train of abuses committed by government against the people, America has the largest contingent of potential patriots in Western history, as very few have been spared. While the list of grievances is sure to grow with time, any delay ensures that we will be reduced in both number and influence with each passing day as the former affects the latter considerably.

The enemy is formidable, as they control the media and seats of government; the former they use to destroy our will and the latter our ability. So when will our situation improve? When the 2nd Amendment is reserved only for those who deprive others of that right? When our numbers are reduced to half of all legal citizens? Shall we wait until all effective means of protecting and preserving ourselves have been destroyed? Our foe may be an imposing figure, but they are no match against nearly 200 million dedicated to the cause of creating liberty and ensuring justice for posterity.

The moral obligation is obvious. We must leave posterity with a natural form of government consisting of a properly functioning constitution, not fabricated government that ignores its most important constitutional duties. Our glorious struggle cannot be achieved by simply moderately altering present laws, for that would leave far too much unfinished business and posterity without the appropriate government in which they are entitled. Not only must laws change but petty politicians must be replaced by grand statesmen.

A severe consequence of unworthy representatives is the loss of our national foundation. No nation can exist without a common history and heritage, which provide the source of any national bond. Government has betrayed this idea through immigration policies that reduce the magnitude of our bond consisting of Christianity in particular and Western civilization in general. As reparation for our priceless loss, we have been forced to support a rise in the standard of living for foreigners both at home and abroad. The more government gives, the more its recipients demand.

Absence of a proper republic ensures that government will turn advantages into disadvantages. No nation has been blessed with such fortune of location, with a neighbor to the north comprised of a citizenry with no intention of harming us and one to the south without the ability. European nations, not being blessed in that regard, were ravaged by centuries of near-constant warfare. Government ignores such a blessing by tempting a myriad of people with legal citizenship at home and pursuing endless war abroad, resulting in hostilities between other nations and within our own. Blessings should be regarded highly, not neglected foolishly.

Only those knowledgeable of their past can predict the future. I see no reason for hope when reflecting upon the past half century in which benefits have been few and trivial while misdeeds are frequent and destructive. We have witnessed our most fundamental rights taken and have received nothing in return. Have they, despite our protests, departed slightly from their course of destruction? No! They only move more quickly! We have been ignored and insulted while witnessing our rights and property taken.

Some will continue to claim that government remains our protector. Only a fool would suppose that the entity that has committed such crimes against us is either willing or capable of such a significant task. Applying common sense to knowledge of recent events makes known the absurdity of their claim. Nothing could be more unfit to protect us than the source of our hardship. It is difficult to solve problems when we are unable to identify them; it is impossible when one is the actual source. Their actions have the dual effect of leaving us more vulnerable while restricting the ability to protect ourselves. As history has shown, conquest often begins with a declaration of friendship.

The United States government has committed treason against its people. Our representatives have initiated a process whereby the term "minority" will accurately describe our status; invited our southern neighbors to massacre fellow citizens; made us allies of the immoral and enemies of the decent; destroyed our property and purchasing power; and diminished our sovereignty both through immigration and global organizations, all while our ability to prevent the continuation of betrayal has deteriorated. In what other manner can we describe government that produces such devastating results in a deliberate manner?

It is often said by the apathetic that politics and current events are avoided due to the low character of those supposedly representing their interests. Politics affects the cost of food and opportunities for their children. Their safety is determined by what they ignore as well as the country they will leave behind. Indifference in serious matters is a sign of weakness. To ignore one's destroyer is to invite one's demise. Such an unfortunate fact makes them the apathetic conquerors of their children's liberty, which they have no right to destroy.

I offer the following challenge with full confidence: name one advantage in continuing our current course. Not a single one can be named. The path to one's demise is never paved with gold.

The consequences, on the other hand, cannot yet be counted or fully understood. Inaction ensures that the path to war at home will continue while peace abroad remains unattainable. We will continue to make enemies with nations who had been our allies while maintaining friendships with those who have committed acts of war against us. The contempt directed against American citizens must become affection, while the ingratitude of our supposed allies must be acknowledged.

Establishing a republic in the distant future would be terribly difficult. Chaos is certain to result from both the number and variety of U.S. citizens. Major conflicts extinguish minor differences. People would ignore minor disputes and celebrate more obvious and important similarities. Success is more easily attained by the strong than the weak, by the numerous rather than the few. We are currently experiencing our worst years, but our foundation consists of an impressive past with remarkable men whom we can look to for guidance.

There is no time better than the present for our response. The continuation of only temporary enjoyment of majorities and the degree to which the people have been oppressed make this time opportune. While we are reduced in number and power daily, the grievances committed against us are more than sufficient to unite and awaken a sleeping giant. If, however, we let this opportunity pass, ourselves and posterity will be subjected to the full will of our internal conquerors.

When George III suppressed American rights, he increased both the severity of the burden and number to whom his scorn was directed. As realized by our founders, obedience to a corrupt government worthy of contempt ensures that freedom will be reduced as time passes. As liberty decreases, so do the means by which the people can protect themselves from the source of their displeasure.

Additional similarities exist between current government and that of King George. Government forms can be broken into two groups: they are either selected by the people or it is forced upon them. The former is our government's designed purpose; allows the people to choose its own representatives and functions as a republican government, while the latter explains government's contemporary function, grants tyrannical power to very few, and resembles a government of succession. The noble purpose of government is irrelevant if it is not executed properly.

The 20th century witnessed a succession of despicable crimes committed against Americans; while causing terrible grief early, the series of injuries grew both in magnitude and frequency. The response after each misdeed was predictable. Each is enacted sooner and with more severity than its predecessor. A single misdeed by government can be an honest mistake, but a continual series of crimes, with a specific beginning, and continuing despite many changes in the names and faces of those who enact and enforce such misguided laws, is proof that a slow, methodical plan that cedes sovereignty first and our nation second has been underway for some time.

That plan will continue until we substantially increase active participation within our movement. Ironically, we must take advantage of four media components that have proven detrimental to our interests:

1. A national radio syndicate available in every market. Great programs currently exist that are not available to everyone: seven weekday programs three hours in length, with one replayed at night. All programs would be hosted by one or more talented supporters of our cause. The programs could differ in format. One could pursue debate from opposing viewpoints in the form of call-in and

scheduled guests. Another may focus entirely on monologues, discussion, and guests representing our philosophy.

2. A cable news channel similar in design but different in substance from its competitors. Guests of opposing viewpoints could be invited, but all hosts would represent our perspective with honesty, integrity, and intelligence. A prime-time show featuring at least two debaters representing conflicting ideas could draw a wide audience. Of course, it would be without the interruptions and short answers that inflict contemporary presidential debates. In an open forum, reason will defeat tyranny every time.

3. A daily newspaper distributed nationally and inspired by the *National Gazette* of the late 18th century. While the radio and television branches of our movement would allow the debate of ideas, the paper would express our philosophy in a factual, informative, and relentless fashion. A large news section would be supplemented by op-ed pages and letters to the editor.

4. A high-quality Web site that would complement the radio station, news channel, and paper is essential. Visitors would have access to live and previous radio shows, highlights of major television footage, and text of major news stories.

These acts must be undertaken. An apathetic people produce corrupt government; an informed and active citizenry demand the opposite. The condemnations against government will be harsh, and some are certain to denounce such behavior as treasonous. Those guilty of such are often the accusers, while innocent parties are the accused. The former confuse treason as acts against immoral government rather than crimes against people.

If we are to surrender our voice to the will of distant bodies, both reason and history must be ignored. When considering our current state, it is clear that the American republic has been abolished. Should ideal government be dissolved and our property confiscated by a group of men in whom we granted no authority? Can anyone argue in favor of the American people being subjected to the will of a few thousand men weaker in mental capacity and physical strength? No single reason exists that can sufficiently support the continuation of our current course. America was founded on the very principle that we must defend today; our will must not be decided by a body so small in number and lacking in morality that sacrifices our freedom in search of empire.

Besides outright admission, government makes mistakes that accidentally reveal their intention. Such was disclosed in 1983 as Martin Luther King, a self-admitted communist, was honored with his own holiday. How could a supposed republic honor a supporter of communism? Although both systems believe influence originates from a particular source, the former cedes such authority to the majority, while the state surrenders none in the latter: a contradiction to say the least.

The idea of re-establishing natural government is likely to surprise both men who believe themselves informed and others who admit otherwise. However, it is a necessary step that we must take for our country, culture, and fellow citizens. Some but not all of the reasons include the following:

1. Sovereignty is partial on the surface and absent in reality. The situation is unacceptable. Natural government can exist when few people represent many, but not when few dictate to the majority. Our pursuit of government representing and defending natural society drifts farther away with each passing day.

2. It is absurd to assume, based upon both action and admission, that government will voluntarily relinquish the authority they have attained.

3. While being subjects, not citizens of government, we must understand that the various crimes committed against us will grow in both number and degree. Apathy ensures inactivity and the further reduction of our national rights.

4. Resistance is the only option in realizing our duty to re-establish liberty. We must band together, laying aside all minor differences, in order to proclaim independence from the

source of our hardship while explaining the necessity of those actions. Additionally, a promise should be made to other nations of the world declaring that we cease all intervention into their affairs, accomplishments that would do more good than every piece of legislation passed over the past half century.

Our current condition of servitude renders freedom for ourselves and liberty for posterity impossible. Government will remain our adversary until we fulfill our duty to reject its unacceptable form and establish one that meets our needs.

The aforesaid may seem surprising to some, but that is due to lack of consideration rather than reason. Time shall make its deliberation more common, and until our sacred duty is pursued, we will simply subsist as those who ignore their most important responsibility, yet understand its urgency, detest its difficulty, wish victory already won, and will be distraught by the fact of its existence.